OCKET GUIDE
The FOUNTAINHEAD

Walter Donway
and
David Kelley, Ph.D.

THE **ATLAS SOCIETY**

Published by The Atlas Society
22001 Northpark Drive, Ste 250 | Kingwood, TX
77339

Cover design by Matthew Holdridge
Book layout by Erin Redding

 AtlasSociety.org

ISBN 978-1-7349605-8-7

Our Mission

The Atlas Society's mission is to inspire people to embrace reason, achievement, benevolence, and ethical self- interest as the moral foundation for political liberty, personal happiness, and a flourishing society.

We build on Ayn Rand's works and ideas and use artistic and other creative means to reach and inspire new audiences. We promote an open and empowering brand of Objectivism; we welcome engagement with all who honestly seek to understand the philosophy, and we use reason, facts, and open debate in the search for truth above all else; we do not appeal to authority or conflate personalities with ideas. We resist moral judgment without adequate facts and believe disagreement does not necessarily imply evasion.

Contents

About Ayn Rand

Ayn Rand was born Alissa Rosenbaum on February 2, 1905, in Saint Petersburg, Russia. Her family was comfortable and prosperous, but from her earliest years, she felt alienated from the grimness of Russian culture. She loved the bright world she saw portrayed in foreign magazines. At the age of nine, she made the conscious decision to become a writer.

Later, she read the works of the greatest romantic writers of the age, especially Victor Hugo. But just as her vision of human potential widened, and the world seemed to open to her, her own world was plunging into disaster. In February 1917, Alyssa witnessed the first shots of the Russian Revolution from her balcony. Soon, communists seized her father's business; her family was reduced to crushing poverty.

She had glimpsed an entirely different world and now conceived a burning desire to flee Russia for the West. As a young woman, she obtained a passport to visit relatives in Chicago and left Russia and her family in January 1926. She would never return. She arrived in New York City after weeks at sea; the skyline of New York City became almost sacred in her life.

She stayed only briefly with her relatives in Chicago, where she selected her American name and pen name, Ayn Rand, and set out for Hollywood. The day after she arrived, she was offered a ride—and then a job as a movie extra—by legendary film director Cecil

B. DeMille. It was not long after, on the set of the film, *King of Kings*, that she met the actor who would become her husband, Frank O'Connor.

For the next decade, Rand worked at odd jobs as did so many heroes of *The Fountainhead* in their early years. She mastered English and wrote screenplays, short stories, and a novel. Her raw talent and perseverance eventually won her production of two Broadway plays and publication of *We the Living*.

The clash of ideas that shape individual lives in *The Fountainhead* echo those Ayn Rand confronted \in her own life and career. Just as the novel's hero, Howard Roark, overcame every obstacle to achieve his highest values, Ayn Rand achieved triumphant success with *The Fountainhead* after a long-fought personal and professional struggle.

She had published *Anthem* and *We the Living* and the play "*Night of January Sixteenth*" but still struggled to make a living during the years of researching and writing *The Fountainhead*. The completed novel was turned down by a dozen publishers until one editor, like the heroes in the novel, staked everything on his independent judgment by threatening to quit if the novel was not accepted. Published, the novel seemed to languish; the tenor of intellectual discussion and literary criticism were not supportive.

These were years when collectivism in the form of Soviet communism and German National Socialism had engulfed European nations. Rand watched with dismay as the same ideas convulsing Europe, gained adherents in America. In *America*, her ideal nation and refuge from communist dictatorship, the same bromides of collectivism, the common man, the arrogance of the creator, and resentment of genius were tearing down the spirit of individualism.

The Fountainhead eventually broke through the prevailing intellectual mindset and by word of mouth became a best-selling novel. Today, more than 6.5 million copies of the novel have been sold. A film was made of *The Fountainhead* starring Gary Cooper and Patricia Neal.

The success of *The Fountainhead* ensured that Ayn Rand's great romantic epic, *Atlas Shrugged*, would be brought out and heavily marketed by a leading publisher.

After the publication of *Atlas Shrugged* in 1957, Ayn Rand devoted herself to nonfiction in essays, columns, and public appearances to elaborate and promote her philosophy. Eventually, these became a series of books applying her philosophy of Objectivism to every crucial controversy in philosophy, culture, education, politics, science, and the arts.

She died in New York City on March 6, 1982.

The *Pocket Guide to The Fountainhead* joins the guide to *Atlas Shrugged* as a resource for readers, educators, and others who seek a concise summary of the plot, characters, and themes of Ayn Rand's great novels. We offer this Pocket Guide as a companion on the life-changing journey of discovering—and creating—the world "as it might and ought to be."

PLOT SYNOPSIS

Ayn Rand defined a novel's "plot theme" as the broadest meaning that integrates the plot's logic. The plot theme of *The Fountainhead* is that fundamental conflicts among individuals arise and are driven by differences in how their minds deal with reality, with life's challenges and choices.

Rand names the four sections of *The Fountainhead* for four individuals distinct in their thinking, motivations, choices, actions, and emotions. These differences are variations on a single psychological theme: independence.

Howard Roark is the man who lives by his own judgment. He will learn, listen, weigh opinions, but in the end his judgment will guide him. In his career, architecture, independence collides with a profession that reveres imitation of historical styles.

Roark's story is his determination to do his own work, his own way, at any price. His brilliantly innovative architecture expresses the logic of the site, materials, structure, and the building's purpose.

From the beginning, he faces opposition of the "second-handers," those whose ideas and opinions are borrowed from others.

Architect Peter Keating is a conformist and social climber who exploits Roark's genius to advance his career.

Ellsworth Toohey is an architecture critic whose life is built upon manipulating others to gain power. He sets his sights on destroying Roark, whose character and talent serve as a living refutation of Toohey's ideals of egalitarianism, worship of the masses, collectivism, and intellectual humility.

Media magnate Gail Wynand, too, lives for power. He is a man of ambition, achievement and taste—but he believes life represents a choice between ruling or being ruled. His drive and genius make him the ruler—but too late he realizes that he has achieved "power" only by subjugating himself to the masses as their voice and servant.

Dominique Francon, a preternatural beauty, grows up with independent judgment and the highest standards, but sees the world as a malevolent realm in which her values have no chance to survive. She loves Roark but cannot bear the idea that the world she despises will destroy him.

The Fountainhead is about Roark's battle to succeed with total integrity. At each crisis, Roark's relationship with the "second-handers" deepens and changes. He does meet men of independent judgment who befriend him, though none consistently and articulately fights for their values as does Roark.

The climax bringing all characters together is Cortlandt Homes—a public housing project. Keating sees the commission as a chance for professional redemption as his career flags. He begs Roark for help. Intrigued by the design challenge, Roark agrees—on condition that his design be implemented without change.

When Roark's agreement with Keating is violated and Roark's innovative plan for Cortlandt is compromised by Toohey's mediocre protégés, Roark decides to make a final, uncompromising statement.

With Dominique's help to ensure no one is hurt, Roark dynamites the first Cortlandt Homes building. In the lead-up to the criminal trial, Wynand, who by now knows and loves Roark, tries to use the "power" he has accumulated to save Roark—only to have the move backfire.

Toohey tries to use the crisis to seize control of Wynand's newspaper empire—and the trial to send Roark to jail.

Responding to Roark's rousing courtroom defense of the role of the innovator as the font of all human progress, the jury acquits him. Wynand's integrity is in shambles—as are Toohey's schemes to destroy Roark—while Keating is left to his own failure.

As his final gesture, Wynand, not born to be a second-hander, commissions Roark to design and build the greatest skyscraper in New York City, the Wynand Building. It will express only Roark's spirit.

Dominique has seen that in triumph and disaster,

11

Roark remains unaffected by the world. She returns to him, realizing it is in reality—not the opinions, prejudices, and weaknesses of other minds—that Roark exists.

The setting of *The Fountainhead* is contemporary with Ayn Rand's writing of the novel: mid-twentieth-century America and the epicenter of the practice of architecture, New York City. Ayn Rand has said that in part she modeled Roark's approach (though not his character) on that of the twentieth-century master of modernism, Frank Lloyd Wright, whose mentor was pioneer architect Louis Sullivan.

Book I: Peter Keating

Howard Roark stands naked on a soaring granite outcropping. Far below is a lake as blue as the summer sky it reflects. Roark is tall with a lean face with cold grey eyes. His hair is exactly the color of a ripe orange.

At the end of his third year at the prestigious Stanton Institute of Technology School of Architecture, Roark has been expelled. He laughs. He knows he must plan his future, but he is happy gazing at the granite, imagining its possibilities for future buildings. Back at the house where he has boarded for three years, he encounters his landlady, Mrs. Keating, who tells him the dean of the Institute wants him to come to his

office. She then boasts about her son, "Petey," who
that day is graduating at the top of his class.

Though his professors of structural engineering and
mathematics were adamant that Roark was a brilliant
man, the professor of design was outraged that Roark
fulfilled every assignment with his own design in his
own style. The dean strives to convince Roark that his
innovations are passing modernist fads, that all great
ideas and styles have already been created.

The dean reminds Roark of his humble beginnings:
Orphaned as a child with no relatives as far as Roark
knows (or cares), he worked his way east from
Ohio with jobs in the building trades, in which he
has worked every summer. Roark is unmoved, and
declines the dean's offer to return in a year.

Leaving campus, Roark reflects that he "never learned
the process of thinking about other people." But he
knows there is an important principle, a "secret," to
explain the difference between himself and the dean.

The same day, Peter Keating is graduating from
Stanton. He is "pale, dark-haired, and beautiful," with
a winning smile. As he sits in the auditorium, he is
keenly aware of those around him—how they might
be seeing him, thinking of him. The commencement
speaker, Guy Francon, the country's most celebrated
architect, laces his remarks with references to the
glorious history of architecture and the need to make
everything secondary to the wishes and tastes of the

client. Keating meanwhile relishes having beaten his classmates for top class honors, even relishing the expulsion of Howard Roark, who'd repeatedly helped Keating with his assignments.

As he walks home, Keating recalls that he once aspired to be an artist, but his mother swayed him to choose architecture because "you meet the best people in it." Keating dismisses the fleeting regret, and lets his mother manipulate him into forgoing a scholarship to study in Paris in order to take a job with Francon in New York City. Roark tells them he is also going to New York City to work for Henry Cameron.

Keating and Roark arrive in New York City, Keating to start work at Francon & Heyer and Roark to "tell Cameron" he is going to work for him. Keating settles at a drafting table but, with his first task, is overwhelmed by panic. Looking around the room at the other draftsmen, however, he convinces himself they are ordinary and relaxes.

Keating begins to establish special relationships with everyone in the office, including Guy Francon. Before long, he becomes Francon's favorite by ferreting out and pandering to his insecurities. He learns that Guy Francon has done no designing since the triumph of the Frink National Bank Building in lower Manhattan, which displays "the entire history of Roman art…" and is considered the greatest building in the city. He devotes himself to social activities that attract new clients.

Three blocks east of the Frink is the Dana Building designed by Henry Cameron. No one notices it today. Its hard, simple lines reflect the steel skeleton as a body expresses its bones. Its only decorations are the long streaks of windows from roof to pavement. Its tenants love the building for its light, air, and logic of design.

Decades earlier, Cameron ranked first, unchallenged, among architects. With the birth of the skyscraper, he was in his element. Then, America's entire conception of architecture began to change, accelerated by the Columbia Exposition of Chicago in 1893. It was ancient Rome on the shores of Lake Michigan, a competition among architects for who could borrow the most from the oldest source. The hugely popular exposition spread across America a wave of new neo-Classical design adopted by every new post office, townhall, and train station.

Now Cameron's firm has been reduced to three rooms in a dilapidated building. Cameron has begun "drinking, quietly, steadily, terribly, for days and nights at a time…"

Roark has walked the city's streets for two days, "his head thrown back," noticing only the buildings. When he says he has come to Cameron about a job drafting, the receptionist goes into Cameron's office, leaving the door half-open. Roark hears Cameron bellow to throw Roark out, then, immediately, to send him in.

Cameron cross-examines Roark: He has not worked anywhere? Stanton expelled him? Cameron laughs crazily. Roark holds out his drawings. Cameron looks at one, then another, then all of them. He curses Roark. He tells Roark to show up at nine sharp. All he can pay is fifteen dollars a week. Again, Cameron calls him a fool for not going elsewhere. He says he'll "kill" Roark if he goes anywhere else.

Francon shows Keating *New Frontiers*, a small magazine, in which a little-known architectural critic, Ellsworth M. Toohey, has written about a Francon & Heyer building. Its long horizontal lines, with string courses on every story, are "the moderating, leveling principle, the lines of equality." Lines of "the people, the great masses." They seem to say "none may rise too high above the restraint of the common level…"

Keating asks about Francon's only daughter, Dominique, nineteen and away at college, but the painful annoyance on Francon's face discourages further inquiry. Keating by now has met partner Lucius N. Heyer, an old man from "an ancient family" important to the firm for his social connections.

That evening, Keating's mind turns to Catherine Halsey. Of all the women he has pursued, she is the one he has an intense desire to see. He understands little about his ease with her, his ability to be completely himself. Orphaned, she has come to New York City to live with her uncle. She is home, as always, when Keating arrives unannounced. They tell each other, simply, that they love one another. Keating is stunned when Katie says her uncle's name is Ellsworth Toohey. He could help Keating immensely in his career. But NOT through Katie, contaminating their relationship with Keating's manipulations and ambition.

Roark has been working for Cameron for several days. He tells Roark to come into his office and fires him. Roark is too good. If Roark were a brilliant exhibitionist going against the crowd, he would not worry. But Roark loves his work. Look at the people in the street. They hate any man who loves his work. Isn't Roark terrified of them? Finally, Cameron says Roark is cruel to make him say it, but does Roark want to end up like Cameron? It is no use striving for an ideal the world will not let him reach. He begs Roark to be reasonable. He makes real to Roark what it means to live the life Cameron has lived. Is that what he wants? Roark says yes. Cameron whispers to Roark that he never has told this to anyone, not in this way.

Keating further ingratiates himself with his boss, and with Lucius Heyer. Given his first building to design, Keating goes to Howard Roark, who redraws the entire structure. He advises Keating that when it comes to the façade, at least do "good classical." Francon is surprised and impressed when Keating presents the work to him.

Henry Cameron receives a letter declining the firm's submission of preliminary drawings and estimates for a new bank building. Hope for this commission had brought Cameron to the office, sober, every day. Called into his office, Roark sees on Cameron's desk a copy of the tabloid *New York Banner*, which panders to readers with tear-jerking stories of unwed mothers, crusades against businesses, quotations from church services, and horoscopes.

Not long after, Cameron collapses. His sister from New Jersey takes him to live with her. Cameron asks Roark to close the office. He warns Roark that the mediocrity reflected in the *Banner* is the world's response to the spirit Cameron and Roark share.

Ellsworth Toohey has become America's most-read architecture critic. His book *Sermons in Stone* has been hailed for its message that there are "no problems, no achievements, no reaches of thought beyond the daily routine of people nameless in the past." The first virtue of architecture is that it is as anonymous "as all greatness." The book now seems to exist in every drawing-room and to be discussed by anyone with intellectual pretensions.

As his years at the firm progress, Keating forgets his struggle with his first building. All clients want is architecture that will impress their friends. At each step, Keating maneuvers to get rid of anyone in his way. First, he begins secretly helping Tim Davis, the top draftsman, with his work, so Davis can spend more time with his new wife. It becomes known around the office and Davis is fired. Keating takes his place.

His next target is Stengel, head designer. Keating knows Stengel's secret ambition is to start his own firm. But Stengel needs the security of at least one good client—which Keating arranges. Keating becomes chief designer.

Reluctantly, he brings his mother to live with him. She does not approve of Catherine Halsey. He decides to visit the latter, as she works around the clock to help Uncle Ellsworth with fan mail related to *Sermons in Stone*. Peter suddenly, urgently asks her if they are engaged. She says yes. But, says Keating, they will keep it secret until Keating is solidly set with Francon & Heyer.

With Cameron's office closed, Keating hires Roark who insists he will do no designing—but work only in the Engineering Department. Keating asks Roark to come out for a drink, to celebrate. When Roark declines, Keating asks why Roark "hates him." Roark doesn't hate him—and Keating finds his indifference even more wounding

At Francon & Heyer, Roark designs structures and interiors, and chokes back his vision of what the buildings could be. Keating begins sneaking Roark into his office to review Keating's work and usually to revise it. Roark despises this, but his impulse is to save the building—as much as he can.

Sent to inspect the progress of buildings under construction, Roark meets a hard-nosed electrician, Mike, who cares only about competence on the job. He soon becomes Roark's first real friend.

Francon calls Roark into his office. He has a client who wants the firm to design a bank building, but he insists that it be modeled on the Dana Building. It's a big step for Roark, says Francon.

Naturally, Francon & Heyer can't put its name on something crazy Modernist, like Cameron's work, but Roark can give it simplicity.

Painfully, Roark asks Francon to let him design as the Dana Building was designed. What difference would it make to Francon since the client wants it? Finally, Roark closes his eyes and says he is begging Francon. Francon says Roark will design according to instructions for the neo-Classical treatment of the façade. When Roark replies that he can't, Francon fires him.

Roark has about run out of other firms to apply. Then, he interviews with John Erik Snyte, who maintains a team of designers and combines the best of their drawings for each project. Roark will be his "Modernist."

Ellsworth Toohey speaks at a union strike against the contractors in the city. Peter goes there to meet Catherine Halsey. Based on the success of *Sermons in Stone*, the *Banner* has hired Toohey to write a syndicated architecture column: "*One Small Voice*." Toohey's speech to the strikers directly opposes the Wynand position on the strike. Toohey rises to explosive applause and addresses the workers as "brothers." His voice has incredible power. "It was the voice of a giant."

Peter sees Catherine beside him "dissolving in the sounds of the loud-speaker." He demands that they leave. She seems to return to herself and agrees.

Austen Heller, a columnist for the conservative *Chronicle*, commissions Snyte's firm to design a house for him. He cannot articulate his yearning for an original home. The firm, as usual, creates an amalgam, but the final version is Roark's design toned down, ornamented, made "cozy." Heller is frustrated. It has so much but it lacks…integrity. Roark grabs the sketch and with a black pencil starts slashing and drawing to restore his plan for the house. Astounded, Snyte fires Roark, but Heller takes the sketch and Roark's arm and says, "We're both fired." At lunch, Heller writes a check to "Howard Roark, Architect," to open an office.

Roark opens his own office and goes to New Jersey to tell Henry Cameron, who is deeply moved and uncharacteristically full of optimism that Roark will succeed. Within a week, Heller knows Roark will be his best friend. The house is completed, but no architectural publication mentions it.

The new crusade of the *Banner*—to be conducted
while publisher Wynand is off on his yacht—is
to attack New York slum lords (secretly, Wynand
corporations want to buy the buildings).
Dominique Francon by now is working for the *Banner*
and a favorite of chief editor Alvah Scarret, who has
built the *Banner* with Wynand almost from the start.
Her assignment will be to investigate slum living.
She moves into one of the slums for two weeks,
bathing in a tin tub of cold water, socializing with
tenants. She writes the story that the *Banner* wants.
But then she gives a talk to a group of social workers,
telling the truth about the laziness, irresponsibility,
and profligacy of the tenants, exactly counter to the
Banner crusade.

Francon sees in the articles that his daughter is
doing what she always does. He is baffled. He hopes
that Peter's "simple wholesomeness" can save her.
Keating first sees Dominique in the firm's reception
room. She is one of the most beautiful women
imaginable with pale gold hair, gray eyes, and
"an air of cold serenity and an exquisitely vicious
mouth." Keating is stunned and begins "revising his
vision of the future," but at the same time senses it
would be better "if he never met her again"—then
begins seeing her regularly. Guy Francon is thrilled.
He strongly hints that the firm soon will need a new

partner. That night, Catherine appears at Keating's apartment. She is flustered, apologetic. Suddenly, Keating sees she is terrified. Something about Toohey made her run out of the apartment. She tells Mrs. Keating that Peter and she are engaged. She wants to marry immediately. Peter says they will get the license tomorrow and marry.

Katie leaves and Mrs. Keating spends the rest of the night browbeating Keating about marrying "a little nobody," damaging his career, alienating Francon. Next day, exhausted, he is at Katie's door. He struggles to tell her this is not the right time. She agrees without a trace of the panic of the evening before.

Suddenly, Keating urges Katie to insist that they marry that day. She laughs. He leaves with the desolate feeling the chance never will come again.

Before the Heller house had been completed, Roark got another small commission for Jimmy Gowan's gas station. Months of idleness follow. Potential clients come, mostly at Heller's insistence, but demand conventional, historical architecture. Roark explains, questions, offers brilliant analogies, urges clients to see through their own eyes. But most often, he concludes, no one is there.

John Fargo, who started as a pushcart peddler, now owns a department store. He wants to revitalize his old neighborhood with a new store. Roark gets the commission.

Whitford Sanborn commissions Roark to design his family's new home, but his wife and the contractor oppose every step. In the end, Mrs. Sanborn won't let the family live there. Only their son, who since college progressively has withdrawn, and is now alcoholic, suddenly declares he loves the house and will live nowhere else. To this house, architectural journals now suddenly pay attention. An architect named Howard Roark was paid $100,000 to design a house, but the family finds it uninhabitable. It is abandoned, "an eloquent witness to professional incompetence."

Lucius Heyer will not die or retire. Francon keeps insisting and Keating, whom Heyer likes, becomes rude. Francon all but promises Keating he will be the next partner.

Then, with dazzling publicity, a worldwide competition is announced to design a new building for Cosmo-Slotnick Pictures of Hollywood. It will be a stupendous skyscraper rising in New York City. Keating works on the preliminary design for weeks, hating the building. When he is finished, he brings the drawings to Roark. Roark redesigns the structure and urges Keating to use "good Renaissance…if there is such a thing" for the façade.

Commissions continue to elude Roark. The Fargo store opens. It cannot save a whole neighborhood, as Fargo hoped, and the building is blamed.

Cameron has a relapse and sends for Roark. Both knowing why. Roark stays for three days. Cameron

seems at peace. He says the only man he hates is Gail
Wynand; that is whom Roark must fight. He knows
what Roark is going through at the office, all of it. He
tells Roark not to be afraid— and to forget what he had
said the day he tried to fire Roark. It was all worth it.

Keating sees Catherine often, but senses the
significance of their meetings is vanishing. Keating
asks her to wait till he wins the Cosmo-Slotnick
competition. Keating also sees Dominique, who
finally lets him kiss her, but her frigidity staggers
him. She apologizes; she has never felt romantic love.
Suddenly, Keating "remembers" she is Francon's
daughter and asks her to marry him. She shudders,
then laughs. If she ever wants to punish herself for
some terrible transgression, she will marry Keating.

Self-doubt plagues Keating: he will lose the Cosmo-
Slotnik competition; Francon will make someone else
partner. He sees only one chance. He goes to Heyer's
apartment. Heyer is frail, his mind feeble. Keating sets
forth how he will blackmail Heyer. Keating escalates
the terror, shouting, until Heyer is trembling, drooling,
and falls to the floor, dead. No one suspects Keating.
Then, Francon calls him to his office. Apparently
recalling Keating's kindnesses and attention, and
having no relatives, Heyer three years ago in his will
left everything to Keating—his interest in the firm,
his fortune, and his porcelain. Keating descends into a
nightmare of horror and guilt.

That lasts only a few days. Keating wins the Cosmo-Slotnik competition to major public acclaim. He is awash in recognition, honors, invitations to speak. He is headline news day after day, often posing with movie stars.

After swearing he would not, he goes to Roark's office. Roark is at the end of his money, with no hope but the decision on one potential commission for a bank building. Keating writes a check for $500; refusing the check, Roark asks only that no one should know he was involved with the Cosmo-Slotnik Building. Keating is wildly indignant—Roark makes him feel ashamed of the building. He hates Roark, always has hated him. Keating deflates, remorseful at his outburst.
Roark gently asks Keating if he is all right to go now.

After the Fargo Store, Roark had gone a long time without a commission, then suddenly Mr. Weidler, a director of the Manhattan Bank, asks him to do preliminary drawings for the bank's new building—a commission that could change everything. Over weeks and weeks of delay, Weidler had been fighting to get Roark's submission accepted. Now, Roark hears from Weidler, who sounds optimistic, and goes to meet with the directors.

They like the structure, but it must have a historical façade. Roark explains the integrity of a building. Yes, the chairman knows that is right, but practically speaking, Roark must accept the terms or not. Roark refuses.

Knowing how much Roark needed the commission, Weidler groans. Why does Roark have to be so selfless?

Roark counters: "That was the most selfish thing you've ever seen a man do."

That evening, Roark asks his friend, Mike, to get Roark a job in the trades. There is one available at Francon's quarry. A few days later, Roark leaves by train for Connecticut, looking back on the New York skyline.

Book II: Ellsworth Toohey

Roark has been at the quarry for two months, drilling in the blazing sun on the granite ledges. He takes pleasure in his physical exhaustion. His pain at the thought of the buildings he is not designing comes infrequently.

Some three miles from the quarry, in the stately Francon country house, Dominique lives in isolation except for a caretaker couple. Amid the luxury, Dominique is aware mostly of her own body, intuiting that around the next corner will be "the sensation of a defiling pleasure."

She walks to the quarry where men labor in the sun. She wears her coolest, sheer green dress. Her eyes rest on Howard Roark's orange hair. He raises his head with a bold look that she experiences as a slap. His is "the most beautiful face she would ever see…the abstraction of strength made visible." She imagines his hand, not the drill, breaking rock. Days later, she encounters Roark on a path and asks why he always stares at her? It would be better if he stopped looking at her. It might be misunderstood. No, says Roark, he doesn't think it would be misunderstood.

Dominique has lost her cherished "freedom." She is compelled to think of Roark and fights to stay away from him. Finally she breaks down: she intentionally damages a tile of her bedroom fireplace, goes to the quarry to find Roark, and asks him to fix it. When he comes that evening, she sits on her bed watching. He looks up, she sees laughter in his expression. He will order the new marble sent to her, then will come and set it. When it arrives, Dominique sends him a note to come that evening. A workman arrives, a squat Italian named Pasquale Orsini. "Red," down at the quarry, sent him to set the tile.

Later she goes to the quarry on horseback to confront Roark. She gallops down the path until she catches him on his way home. Why didn't he come to set the marble?

Did it make any difference to her who came?

She lashes his face with her whip and spurs her horse away.

Three days later, as she sits in her bedroom late at

night, the French doors open, Roark enters and, after a passionate struggle, takes her sexually. After he leaves, she rushes for the bathroom to wash but cannot bear to relinquish traces of his body on hers.

The next night, Roark receives word that oil magnate Roger Enright has been trying to locate him. Roark is on a train to New York City in half-an-hour.

When Dominique returns to the quarry, Roark is gone. The superintendent tells her he has left. If she doesn't know his name, she can't find him. She does not ask; she walks away. "It is her last chance at freedom." In a thin envelope with the masthead of the *Banner*, Ellsworth Toohey has sent Keating proofs of tomorrow's column, lauding the Slotnick Building as a tribute to collectivism: the masses, equality, and collective unity. Later that day, Keating hears that someone has just shot Toohey. He is panicked, but soon learns the gunman, sculptor Steven Mallory, missed.

When Keating meets Toohey, he is surprised by the contrast between the booming voice from the lecture hall and the critic's frail physical frame: "his thin little body…like that of a chicken emerging from the egg."

Toohey subtly mocks Keating, then laughing. Keating feels increasingly comfortable with Toohey's apparently non-judgmental understanding. When Toohey praises the structural design and layout of the Cosmo-Slotnick design, Keating senses Toohey knows he did not design it.And he sees approval in Toohey's eyes. Toohey congratulates Keating on his engagement to his "niece Little Catherine," then belittles it. Toohey invites Keating to tea with Katie. Toohey is dressed with exquisite taste, and Keating wishes Katie did not wear the same suit for the third season. She seems heavy, colorless, tired. Toohey again humorously derides the prospect of marriage. Katie has started working with children in a settlement house; Toohey approves.

Keating has seen a newspaper notice and drawing of the Enright House, combining severe mathematical order with "free fantastic growth." Toohey seems not to recognize the name, "Roark," despite his photo plainly displayed in the paper. But when Keating mentions his connection with Roark, Toohey sharply cross-examines him. Does Roark laugh often? No. Does he ever seem unhappy? Never. Does he like to be admired? No. Does he believe in God? No. Keating is innocently saying what he knows about Roark; Toohey recognizes the threat Roark's individualism and creativity pose.

Keating meets with Lois Cook, whose incoherent writings Toohey has praised publicly and extravagantly. She wants a private residence, a shrine on the Bowery. A cynic who understands Toohey's assault on standards, she wants her house to be the ugliest in the city. Keating accepts the commission. His design becomes the most published, reproduced drawing he ever did. In his better moments, he is ashamed.

Dominique has returned to New York, often taking solitary walks. She always hated city streets, faces filled with a nameless fear, "ready to pounce on whatever was held sacred" by anyone else. She hates that the man from the quarry is shared by them. Back in the *Banner* office, she sees the sketch of the Enright House. She tells Toohey that the man who designed it should commit suicide. Something this beautiful should not exist to be desecrated by people living in it.

At Steven Mallory's trial, Toohey pleas for leniency. Only Mallory is unmoved by Toohey's dramatic "selfless" gesture. Mallory gets two years, sentence suspended.

At the first meeting of eighteen architects in Toohey's home, Keating is the only architect of distinction except for Gordon Prescott. Keating can't figure out why these others are here. He is elected chairman; the group will be called the Council of American Builders. Toohey calls for a crusade for "the underprivileged and unsheltered." Dominique arrives toward the end of the meeting, observing the group with disdain. She leaves with Peter, who recognizes that her former indifference to him has become revulsion. She rebuffs his request to see her again.

Roger Enright, who started his career as a coal miner, had hired Roark on the spot. Before the construction of the Enright House begins, Joel Sutton, planning a huge office building, summons Roark. Heller wants Roark to attend a party at the home of Ralston and Kiki Holcombe; Joel Sutton will be there. Roark resists until Heller says that Francon and his daughter will be there, as well.

"I'll go." It will be the hardest way for Dominique to realize that the architect she admires is the man in the quarry. With Heller's introduction, they correctly greet each other. Dominique cannot help saying "the Enright House…" She searches Roark's face for any hint of a personal expression. She feels mocked.

Dominique watches him all evening, delivered to the crowd, to any person who wants to own him. And he knows, she is sure, this is harder than watching him under the blazing sun in the quarry.

Ellsworth Toohey also sees Roark. As Toohey walks through the crowd, his eyes keep returning to Roark. For the rest of the evening, he never lets his view of Roark be obstructed for a moment.

Dominique's column in the *Banner* attacks the Enright House and Roark, saying that the city and its buildings, by comparison, will be made ugly and small. Toohey comes to her office. He knows exactly what she is saying. Toohey makes real and vivid the pain that Roark must have felt year after year, unrecognized while his inferior Keating succeeds. Dominique leaps to her feet, shaking, and screams for him to get out.

Dominique decides she must stop Roark before the world destroys him and his genius. The world does not deserve him, nor will it permit him to survive. When Roark's potential new client, Joel Sutton, asks her opinion of Roark, she talks him out of signing the contract with Roark. The architect he needs is Peter Keating.

That evening, Dominique comes to Roark's apartment unannounced. She tells him she will take from him every commission she can; she will try to destroy him, starve him. When she has hurt him, she will come to him. She has nothing to offer; she wants sex like "a whore, a cat on a fence."

She starts to tell Roark she loves him, but he stops her.

Toohey hears of Dominique's new social whirl to steal clients from Roark. Toohey reveals his animus against Roark for achieving what few can aspire to achieve. Roark is revealing to people, Toohey says, what they are, their limitations. Dominique continues her campaign to switch clients from Roark to Keating. And each night she succeeds, she comes to Roark's apartment. They have agreed never to be seen together in public. At one point, she tells Roark that everything she has done in her life is because of a world that would make him work in a quarry.

He knows that.

Ellsworth Toohey was born a sickly child, physically weak but with a keen mind, especially the ability to understand people and the weaknesses he could use to manipulate them. His weapons are his scholarship, rhetorical skills, psychology, and unbounded altruism and pity. Initially attracted to religion, he adopts socialism as a better tool for undermining strength and success.

Graduating from Harvard, he comes to New York City as a career counselor advising that people avoid the selfish choice of careers they love. The success of *Sermons in Stone* leads to a column at the *Banner*, where he also helps editor-in-chief Alvah Scarret fill positions, little positions that no one cares about. He creates a cadre of *Banner* employees—not a "union," a mere club. He creates councils with a celebrated chairman, the members undistinguished. The builder's council signs a statement that they are "servants of the proletariat." The label upon which he insists for himself is "humanitarian."

Dominique visits every one of Roark's buildings in or out of town, never mentioning it to him. He is winning commissions, including a fifty-story skyscraper for Wall Street prodigy Anthony Cord. That summer, Kent Lansing comes to Roark for a luxurious hotel on Central Park South. Despite bureaucratic opposition and Dominique's every effort, Roark gets the commission. Dominique is secretly pleased that Roark may be winning. But Toohey is alarmed, and hatches a plan to ruin Roark.

Toohey convinces millionaire Hopton Stoddard,

who reveres Toohey's otherworldliness, to build an interdenominational temple to the human spirit. Stoddard must use Howard Roark as the architect, but Roark must never know of Toohey's involvement. With Toohey's extensive coaching, Stoddard convinces Roark to take the commission, then leaves on a year-long world pilgrimage. There must be huge publicity for the project, Toohey insists, but the building must be concealed from the public entirely.

Next day, Toohey walks into Dominique's office to tell her. But what is Toohey after? He is going to make Roark famous.

After a long search, Roark chooses Steven Mallory, the man who shot at Toohey, to create a statue of a naked woman as the focal point of the temple. When Roark finds Mallory and meets him, Mallory has been almost broken, emotionally, by the response to his art and his treatment by clients. Roark shows complete confidence in him, the highest respect for his work, and offers him the best possible contract. When Roark suggests Dominique Francon as the model, Mallory believes it will be impossible to get her.

They will, says Roark, and Dominique agrees. She faces the indignation of Guy Francon, the pleas of Keating, and Toohey's displeasure. Oh, Dominique tells Toohey, she told Roark who was behind Stoddard's choice of Roark. Why, asks Toohey? Because she saw the drawings. That good, asks Toohey? Better, she says.

35

And what did Roark do? He laughed. Toohey nods. Others soon will join Roark in laughing.

That winter, Roark pours his energy into the Stoddard temple. Roark, Mallory, Mike, and Dominique become friends and, as spring arrives, and the temple rises, spend many evenings together in the construction site shack.

In May, work on the Aquitania, the hotel project Kent Lansing won for Roark, halts. Two investors lost everything in the stock market crash of 1929.

As Toohey planned, the Stoddard Temple explodes into a scandal. Returning from his trip, Stoddard and Toohey tour the building. Toohey says it has turned out to be a sacrilegious insult to the spirit of religion, glorifying man rather than God. With the nude statue, it is more like a brothel. The project failed disastrously, Toohey says, because God rejected Stoddard and his gift. Now, Stoddard must sue Roark for malpractice and damages and use the money to convert the temple to a home for subnormal children, a humble gift God might accept.

Dominique asks Toohey what he's after. Won't the scandal pass in a few months? Precisely, says Toohey. It will be a dead issue, all the reasons and arguments forgotten, but everyone will recall that someone called "Howard Roark" created a scandal, was sued, cheated the client, and, above all, is a hater of religion.

The *Banner*, Wynand away on his yacht, crusades

against the temple. Roark declares he will defend himself in court. Most big names in architecture, including Keating, testify that Roark is incompetent, inexperienced, and malicious. Toohey locates in the morgue of the *Banner* the photograph of Roark exulting as he looks at the Enright Building. It runs with the caption: "Happy, Mr. Superman?"

The last to testify is Dominique. She replies for the plaintiff with heavy irony. The temple is built to the highest in the human spirit, to man's rising, man's self-esteem and pride. How could Roark inflict that on people? How could he leave them to feel totally inadequate—and call it religion?

Then, the defense is called. Roark walks to the judge with an envelope of 10 photographs of the temple and says that the defense rests. Roark loses the suit and must pay to alter the temple.

Dominique writes her *Banner* column with the same irony as her testimony. Dominique tells Scarret to print it or she will quit. He fires off a telegram to ask Wynand what to do. The reply is "Fire the bitch! G.W." Toohey gets a copy and presents it to Dominique.

Catherine has become a social worker. Now, she's unhappy—and worse, she is beginning to hate people. Toohey replies that she is only concerned with herself and her own happiness. She is unhappy, Toohey says, because she is egoistical.

The next evening, Peter Keating comes to visit. It has been six months since Keating has seen her and only a few times in the last three years. He asks her why they haven't married?

Yes, they are going to get married. He will be back at nine in the morning. After he has left, she lies on the bed sobbing. Toohey walks in. She raises her head and without thinking blurts out: "I'm not afraid of you, Uncle Ellsworth!"

That evening, Dominique arrives at Keating's apartment. Without preliminaries, she asks Keating if he will marry her. It must be tonight. Without discussion. They can drive to Connecticut, marry, and be back in three hours. What are her reasons? She once told him. If he doesn't have the courage to recall them, don't expect her to repeat them. All right, Dominique, Keating says.

Back in the city, she drops him at his apartment. Everything, she says, will begin tomorrow. She goes to Roark's apartment; they make love most of the night; she tells Roark that she loves him, and that she married Peter Keating. The Stoddard trial has renewed her fear of the world.

Marriage to Keating is her rebellion.. She loves Roark too much to see him destroyed. She will destroy herself first.

Roark won't try to stop her. He loves her as selfishly as he loves the fact that he exists. But if he married her, now, he would become her whole existence. She would surrender to him because he demanded it and it would destroy her and their love. He kisses her and lets her go.

The next morning, Keating is locked in his room trying to forget that Catherine is waiting. Dominique arrives at noon. She takes charge. She wants nothing to change. Mrs. Keating must stay with them. As word of the marriage spreads, Keating gets calls of congratulations. People drop by the apartment that evening; Dominique is the perfect hostess. After they leave, Dominique tells Peter to come on and "get it over with." Her body has no response, not even revulsion. Keating asks: "Who was he?" "Howard Roark." He thinks she is joking.

The Stoddard Temple is remodeled as "The Hopton Stoddard Home for Subnormal Children." Catherine Halsey is put in charge of occupational therapy and moves into the home as a permanent resident. She takes up the work with a fierce zeal. She is belligerent, speaking of "human reclamation." She is elated at every tiny achievement of the least able children.

Dominique's statue had been sold. No one knows that Ellsworth Toohey purchased it.

Long after it is remodeled, Roark goes one evening to see the Stoddard building. Suddenly, he sees Ellsworth Toohey. They are alone here, says Toohey. No one can hear. Roark can tell Toohey in any words he wishes what he thinks of Toohey.

"But I don't think of you."

Book III: Gail Wynand

In his penthouse in a Mid-Manhattan hotel he owns, Gail Wynand stands with a gun to his temple. He can't pull the trigger because he feels nothing—no dread, despair, relief. At fifty-one, he is publisher of the powerful New York *Banner*, a nationwide newspaper chain, and an investment empire.

He reflects that the day had been ordinary, working at the *Banner*, his attention on every detail of the *Banner* and papers nationwide. He terrifies editors with sudden calls and frequent threats.

Why have references to a novel by Lois Cook, *The Gallant Gallstone*, satirizing egoism, been popping up in the *Banner* for weeks? Who is behind it? Well, says an editor, it may be Ellsworth Toohey. Stop him.

Later, Toohey comes to his office. He would like to recommend an architect for Wynand's big new housing project, Stoneridge—a rare mega-project in the Depression. Toohey recommends Peter Keating. He asks Wynand to give half-an-hour to Mrs. Peter Keating. Toohey has taken the liberty of sending Wynand a present.

Returning home, Wynand has forgotten the present. He has dinner with a beautiful woman and abruptly tells her they are finished. Feeling empty, he thinks back on his life.

He grew up abjectly poor on Manhattan's west side in Hell's Kitchen, at the time a dangerous waterfront district. The only outlet for his ambition was as a gang leader. On the odd jobs at which he worked, his quick mind came up with ideas for improvement, but the response was, "You don't run things, here." He taught himself to read and began reading everything, using his gang to steal library books.

At 16, looking over the city at night, wondering what is in every home, Wynand answers: the newspaper. That is the direction he chooses. Against all odds, he begins, scorning help in his poverty, and in two years is an associate editor. He obtains ownership of his first newspaper by putting the gangsters who own it in the penitentiary. He calls it the New York *Banner*.

An element of idealism had fueled his ambition at first, but experience led him to believe that integrity is impossible; he resolved to seek power, instead. In some cases, he invests a great deal in destroying someone—especially those who boast the highest and unshakable ideals. "You can't escape human depravity," he tells them.

At thirty-five, he heads Wynand Enterprises. His luxury yacht is the "I Do." Because now Wynand does run things around here. The only non-public aspect of his life or soul, the only thing still sacred, is his totally private art collection.

He goes to his study and sees Toohey's present: It is Mallory's statue of Dominique Francon. He stands looking at it for an hour, then calls Toohey and tells him to come over.

Wynand says he hates getting the statue from Toohey. Is Toohey offering him this statue if he interviews Mrs. Peter Keating? No, says Toohey, this *is* Mrs. Keating.

Oh, you damn fool, says Wynand. Doesn't Toohey realize that the sure way to kill Wynand's interest in the statue is to meet the model? You haven't seen her, says Toohey. All right, Wynand will see her.

Dominique and Peter have been married for 20 months. She has slipped seamlessly into his life, as hostess, social secretary, homemaker. She is perfect, attentive, and always agreeable. She brought nothing but her clothes and changed nothing in any detail. She is utterly unresponsive in bed and Keating tries less and less often. She never expresses a thought or wish of her own. One evening he confronts her about it: there's no "real *you*," no self. "Where's your I?" Where is yours? she replies. For a moment, she is tender as Peter begins to understand, perhaps a first step in recovering a real self. Then, Toohey calls and the moment passes.

Toohey comes to talk about the Stoneridge project and says Dominique should call Wynand. Meeting in his office, Wynand is astounded to discover this is the Dominique Francon who once worked for him. What is her pitch for Peter Keating? There is no reason Wynand should hire him unless he wants to sleep with her.

Wynand accepts, astonished by her honesty. They will go on a two-month yacht cruise. When they return, she can go back to Keating with the Stoneridge contract. Two days before they sail, Wynand shows her his private art collection. No one else ever has seen it. The statue is there. On the cruise, Wynand treats Dominique with great gallantry. The yacht is the truest luxury she has ever experienced. At the first dinner, they begin to see themselves in each other. Dominique finally says that when she listens to him, she hears her innermost self speaking. He keeps saying, in an impassioned way, things she never expected to hear. And keeps seeing in Dominique things she never expected to be seen. Standing with her on the deck, Wynand tells her he loves her and asks her to marry him.

She is conflicted. She has tapped the idealism he has buried in pursuit of power, making him unsuitable for her quest to erase herself. But then thinks back to the Stoddard Temple and asks if he means "Mrs. Wynand Papers?" Yes, she will marry him. He says they will not make love until they are married.

When they return much earlier than expected and tell Keating, he says at first he doesn't care about the contract. Then, bitterly, he says that if Dominique and Wynand want to act like truck drivers, why should Keating not use them both? Keating gets the contract for Stoneridge and a "bonus" check for a quarter-million dollars. Dominique will go to Reno the next day.

Before she departs, Dominique asks Steven Mallory where Roark is doing his latest job. Mallory's new

43

apartment is spacious, filled with items he has chosen, because of Wynand's patronage of his art.

She gets off the train to Reno at the small town where Roark is working. She walks through the night to find the construction site. She passes windows and shudders to think how anyone looking out any window might see Roark; the world she hates can have him, but she cannot. The building site is still lit up. Roark is there. She makes a desperate plea that they marry; he would give up architecture and they would live in some small town. Roark explains why that soon would fail. He tells her to stay married to Wynand and stop torturing herself. He won't let her stay the night; he walks her back to the train.

Keating's spirit is declining. He has lost Dominique through a shabby bargain; he has lost interest in building. He turns to Toohey for reassurance, giving him $10,000 for any charity and begging Toohey to say that this is what makes a man good. Toohey worms out of him that Dominique and Gail Wynand are going to marry. Toohey and Alvah Scarret want to stop it.

Toohey points out that Wynand is not "like them." Now, Dominique, also not like them, is added to the formula, increasing the threat. For Toohey and Scarret, says Toohey, working at the *Banner* will be much more dangerous. They must be close allies in all things.

At the Council of American Writers, Toohey declares they will make a new play by one of their members, "No Skin Off Your Ass," a hit. Jules Fougler, the celebrated drama critic Toohey got hired by the *Banner*, pronounces it "a great play." Members of the group, they agree, have no chance to be playwrights if the works of Henrik Ibsen are the standard. The little guy has no chance if not born with the "glandular accident" of talent. But if "No Skin Off Your Ass" is acclaimed, then people will lose their ability to recognize greatness. Everyone will have an equal chance. Keating arrives and takes comfort in their company.

Returning from Reno, Dominique demands a formal extravaganza of a wedding—suitable to the publisher of the *Banner*. Wynand had wanted it private but complies. The wedding with 600 guests and "haystacks of lilies" is as exhibitionist as Dominique demanded. Wynand is aloof and distinguished, celebrating inside himself the marriage he wanted.

In Wynand's penthouse for the first time, Dominique feels at home and at peace. They do not leave it for two weeks; Wynand does everything possible to make it unnecessary for Dominique ever to leave.

Toohey and Scarret discuss the "new Wynand." Scarret says Wynand is working harder than ever and seems happy. Toohey says that happiness is the most dangerous thing that could happen to Wynand.

Dominique will not let him forget who he is. She gets tickets to "No Skin Off Your Teeth" (the changed title, as Toohey writes, a concession to middle-class sensibilities). Dominique says the *Banner* made the play a great hit. Wynand replies that he never apologizes for the *Banner*. The play is awful, but the audience came prepared by Fougler. Dominique presses Wynand on the play, which he hated, and the role of the *Banner*. She goes after Wynand relentlessly, contrasting his remark to her about "the highest in man" with bits of the play. He should buy the original manuscript and put it on a pedestal in his art collection. He should force Dominique to play one of the characters.

Dominique and Wynand go on another summer cruise. He is more and more in love with her and articulates her meaning to him. She is the only one whose outside matches perfectly her inside. This is integrity. And that is what he lacks, says Wynand. It is impossible in people, he says, but Dominique wants it. He confesses that breaking men of integrity was his way to confirm his choice to pursue power. Despite her disdain for that choice, Dominique sees that it comes from the same view of the world as her own. We have a great deal in common, she tells him: "We've committed the same treason somewhere."

For many weeks, when alone, they share a silence of understanding. He declares his absolute life-giving need for her. It might be Roark speaking. She is afraid, she says, of what she is doing to him. She doesn't love him. Wynand says he can't even care about that. He loves Dominique with such an intense and absolute love that his own love has become the point: "The ability to desire like that." A sense of exaltation.

Book IV: Howard Roark

On a spring morning, a young man is bicycling
through rural Pennsylvania. The golden green of
early spring, the sun through the leaves, give him joy.
He is full of high ideals, with the spirit captured by
great music, but recently has graduated from college
discouraged with the view of life he encountered—
and the view of life he sees in towns and cities. He
wishes that what man created gave him the exalted
feeling nature gives him this spring day.

From the crest of a hill he sees buildings in the valley
below. He stops, shocked at their beauty, how they
complete the landscape and enhance it; they are small
houses, no two alike, but variations on a theme like a
symphony. A man sits on a nearby boulder. The boy
approaches him and asks if this possibly can be real.
Yes, the man says; it is now. It is Howard Roark. Who
built it? Roark did.

After a long silence, the boy says only "thank you."
In those words, Roark hears profound gratitude, but
cannot know that he has given the boy "the courage
for a lifetime."

Roark got the commission to build this resort,
Monadnock Village, from Caleb Bradley, a
real-estate investor. Roark senses something strange
about the commission, especially how the investors
easily accepted his having built the Stoddard Temple,
but he accepts when he gets free rein to design it. It

will be an affordable place for middle-income people to vacation with privacy and natural beauty as a respite from city life. With draftsmen from his former office and Mike and Mallory, he works for a year on the gigantic project. All feel exhilarated by it.

Just as it is finished, Kent Lansing calls; he finally owns the Aquitania Hotel project. He is ready for Roark to finish the job. Roark has been working steadily on projects around the country, but this will be his first job in New York since the Stoddard Temple.

Months later, Bradley and his core investors are arrested for fraud. They sold two hundred percent ownership of Monadnock Village. The scheme was to pick the least attractive location and the worst architect, in the expectation it would go bankrupt and they would never have to pay out earnings. Instead, by word of mouth, then magazine stories, the resort became overbooked and revenues flowed in.

Austin Heller writes a passionate article on the scandal and the injustice to Roark, which sparks publicity for his work. Businessmen are impressed that Monadnock made money despite the investors' intent. Roark is winning customers one individual at a time. He moves his offices to the top floor of the Cord Building.

A few months later, Gail Wynand invites Roark to his office. At the meeting, each is stunned by the recognition of another self; each exchange seems to surprise them both and bring them closer together.

Wynand wants to build a house in the country; every time he has seen a house he liked, Roark has been the architect. Wynand wants to build a house because he loves his wife. He does not want to share her with the world. He wants a fortress, prison, treasure vault, and temple. It must be so beautiful they don't want to leave. Wynand says Roark must meet his wife to fully understand. Does Dominique know he has selected Roark, he asks? No, it is Wynand's idea to express his love for Dominique. Roark takes the commission.

At his office, Wynand reads everything in the *Banner* morgue about Roark. Mostly, it is about the Stoddard Temple. Wynand never saw the drawings, photos, and has not known till now that Roark was the architect. He reads about the *Banner* campaign, the trial, and spends an hour gazing at the drawings.

They drive to the 500-acre plot in Connecticut that Wynand has purchased. Seemingly despite himself, Wynand opens up, revealing about his life and what the *Banner* has meant to him; and expressing regret about what the *Banner* did to Roark. Roark suggests no blame, including the Stoddard Temple. Wynand has revealed too much of himself, though, and retreats into silence. When he drops Roark at the Cord building, he says with "offensive formality" that Mr. Roark should do the design, and not contact Wynand unless it is unavoidable.

When Roark has finished the drawings, he brings them to Wynand, who accepts the design but then tries to break Roark as he has broken the integrity of other men. You want very much to build this? Yes, Roark says. Then, here is the deal. It will be built exactly as designed. Roark will sign a contract to be the sole builder of all Wynand real-estate ventures— the largest such architecture opportunity in America. Roark will design in any style requested: Greek, Gothic, Renaissance. He will please the public. He will become in architecture what Wynand has become in journalism—the dominant power, famous, rich. If Roark does not agree, Wynand will ensure Roark never builds again. No potential employer can withstand Wynand's pressure. The quarry? That will be closed to him, also.

Sure, says Roark "gaily." He grabs a pencil and paper from Wynand's desk and quickly and expertly sketches the Wynand house with all classical decorations. It is not a parody; it is a rendering that architects would applaud. Is that what you want? As a tribute to your love for your wife? Wynand's face drops to his desk. Good God, no! He has met his match in Roark's understanding of Wynand's deeper integrity.

Wynand wants Roark to meet Dominique that evening for dinner. Before Roark arrives, Wynand shows her the sketch of the house. There can be no mistake about the architect. If Wynand were watching her and Roark in bed, "the violation would be no less terrible." Dominique and Roark conduct themselves formally. They stand around the drawings discussing the details. Dominique can't believe they expect her ever to live in the house.

Now, in his *Banner* office, editing proofs of the next day's stories, Wynand feels disgusted at the phrases, like chewing gum spat out, stepped on, picked up, and rechewed… He thinks of Howard Roark and it makes the job easier. He sees Roark again and again—in the penthouse, Roark's office, Roark's apartment. Wynand talks about his earliest years, the fights, his disgust at the world around him, his impatience with incompetence—and the pursuit of power as his solution. We are as different as two men can be, says Wynand. He once thought so, says Roark, remembering Cameron's hatred of the *Banner* as a symbol of the evil that destroyed him and would destroy Roark. But not now.

As the days pass, Dominique feels she is doing the hardest thing Roark ever demanded of her. The way Roark looks at her says nothing has changed. She stands aside and watches Roark and Wynand together. She is no longer afraid that Roark will be destroyed. She feels the peace of finality, free from her fear of the world. Now, she must wait patiently for Roark to reclaim her.

Wynand summons Toohey to his office. The only picture on the wall facing his desk is the photograph of Roark's exultation at the Enright House opening.

The *Banner* ran it with the caption, "Are you happy, Mr. Superman?" Wynand tells Toohey never again to use Roark's name   in his column. And to keep "One Small Voice" small—very small. Toohey agrees and leaves. He is   confident his power at the *Banner*—and in the culture—is safe.

Toohey is at a gathering of his wealthy supporters, reading his new "One Small Voice" column. The theme is that great confusion is caused by seeing freedom and coercion as opposites. In fact, with every new coercion comes new freedom. Look at traffic lights freeing us from traffic accidents. Only with complete coercion comes complete freedom.

That's right, shrieks Mitchell Layton, as he finishes reading. Layton inherited a quarter billion dollars and has spent his life trying to make amends for it. Toohey talked him into buying a sizeable stake in the *Banner*. Layton is concerned about a "We Don't Read Wynand" campaign, but Toohey urges him to bide his time.

Toohey listens to people voicing the other views he has promoted: unselfishness is the moral ideal; reason is oppressive; there's no such thing as a person, only collective identity. He has a vision of a huge typewriter, each key representing one of the famous names he hears at the meeting. His fingers control the keyboard because he created the career and fame of every one of them.

Keating is using his own fortune to keep his firm running. He doesn't know why it has failed so rapidly; other firms are surviving the depression. He doesn't understand how the public now responds to architecture but senses a kind of nihilism in architects like Gordon L. Prescott, chairman of Toohey's Council of American Builders.

Keating walks slowly; he has gained weight; his face is swollen, its lines a blur; and his hair is graying. He is 39. He has brought his mother back to live with him. She wonders where he goes every other weekend, letting no one know what he does. Keating has a shack in an obscure village as an art studio. He has returned to the unborn ambition of his youth. It leaves him at peace even though he realizes his work is mediocre.

Neil Dumont, his partner, forces Keating to think of Toohey. Everyone knows that Toohey can select the architect for the biggest project in the country, the vast public housing project in Astoria called Cortlandt Homes. Dumont says it would save the firm, restore Keating's reputation. Keating goes to Toohey. He asks him why he now mentions only Gus Webb in his column? Toohey insists it always was clear he did not back individuals; change is the principle of the Universe.

Toohey knows Keating came to talk about Cortlandt Homes. Keating is honest about what it would mean.

But, says Toohey, this is no ordinary government project; it is to be a model for the country and the world. It cannot be another over-budget fraud. The architect who designs the project must achieve supreme economies to make units available at fifteen dollars a month—a huge challenge to engineering, design, materials, and building methods. In truth, says Toohey, he recommended Prescott and Webb—and others who submitted preliminary plans. They did not pass muster on the extreme economy required. If Keating can even get close, Toohey will back him to the hilt.

Keating spends the next day and night reviewing specifications for Cortlandt Homes. He calls Roark's secretary for an appointment.

Keating tells Roark he knows he is a parasite. He has fed on Roark and all the men like him. With a new kind of honesty, he says he needs the prestige he doesn't deserve for an achievement he didn't accomplish to save a reputation he has not earned. It is his last chance: Cortlandt Homes. Roark knows all about it. Keating tells him about the meeting with Toohey, and leaves the specifications on Roark's desk.

The next day Keating returns, and Roark says he will do it. He has been working on the problems of low-rent housing for years—not to help the poor, or to save Keating, but because of the potential of modern materials, modern products, for building cheaply, intelligently. Did Keating say the units must rent for fifteen dollars? Roark will show him how to do it for ten dollars. In all the years he worked on this problem, he neither hoped nor expected to be able to demonstrate at scale what he could do. He knows he will never be given a job by any government employee. He could not get past Toohey. Or any group or committee. That is why Roark needs Keating.

But there are conditions. Roark loves this work. He wants to see Cortlandt erected—to see it whole, clean, integrated, unbroken. He wants to design Cortlandt and to see it built exactly as he designs it. He can pass up the money and credit for the work, but the work itself cannot be compromised.

Keating would sell his soul for the project. No, says Roark, that is the easiest thing in the world. Does Keating know what it would mean to keep his soul? Keating says he knows it will be terribly difficult to overcome interference by petty demands for changes. Roark says Keating won't succeed unless he realizes that Roark is giving him a sacred trust. Roark will have only Keating's word. Keating gives his word. They sign a contract stating the full agreement. It will have no legal validity. But Roark could make it public. If Keating's courage fails at any point, he will know that if he gives in, he will lose everything. Everyone would say you're a fool, says Keating. He is getting everything. But no, he says, he knows that Roark is getting even more: the challenge and joy of building. Roark sees that understanding as a triumph for Keating and invites him to stay for a drink to celebrate.

Before he leaves, Keating has something to show Roark. He hasn't shown his paintings to anyone. Roark looks at them for a long time. He says, gently, that it is too late. Keating nods. He knew that. When Keating is gone, Roark leans against the door, closing his eyes, sick with pity. He has never felt this before, never felt this uncleanness. There is shame in the feeling that he should pronounce judgment upon a man where there could be no shred of respect. He reflects that this monstrous feeling, pity, the world calls a virtue.

Dominique has accepted living in the completed house. It is designed entirely around her, even her height, the shade of her skin. When she lies in bed with Wynand, she feels she is getting pleasure from both men. She knows she belongs to Roark as she never belonged to Wynand. But Wynand feels the house is exactly what he wanted: Dominique safe, away from the city, only for him. Roark is the only guest permitted there.

Plans for Cortlandt Homes show six buildings, each fifteen stories high, with the greatest possible sunlight and air, innovative internal efficiencies in building and maintenance, and flexibility for each apartment. When Keating shows them to Toohey, he glances at them and howls with laughter. He knows at a glance that Roark designed it. Keating has achieved what Toohey has sought for a lifetime and what men for centuries have sought in battles. He has harnessed genius. Keating tells Toohey it will rent for ten dollars a unit. Toohey has not the slightest doubt. The plans will go through, Keating will be the architect.

When Wynand sees the *Banner*'s spread on Cortlandt Homes, he curses and throws a copy of the *Banner* at Roark. Wynand doesn't need to see Roark's signature. Roark says that Peter Keating designed this. He will say no more.

Wynand has told every department and editor to mention Roark's work on every occasion. Then, Wynand edits every word of it. He tells Dominique that all the power he has worked to achieve now will give Roark the public support and recognition he deserves. And Wynand uses all his clout to get commissions for Roark.

One morning, Wynand leads Roark to Hell's Kitchen and a five-block area of utter decay. He will build there the largest and tallest skyscraper in the city. Roark will be the architect. Roark is shocked. It will be by far the greatest building in New York City and the masterpiece of Roark's career. It is the best gift Wynand can offer to the man in the world who has meant most to him.

"There it is, Howard, across the street. Yours—from me."

Walking home one evening, Keating runs into Katie. She is working in Washington; they have not seen each other in years, not since he abandoned her on the day they were to marry. Keating says it's pointless to say he's sorry. But, at least Katie should acknowledge that he hurt her. Oh, yes, when Peter didn't show up to take her to get married, she sobbed and screamed "some horrible things" at Uncle Ellsworth. He had to have her sedated.

Keating says not marrying her was the worst thing he did in his life. The worst was not hurting her. Marrying her was the one thing he wanted in his whole life. People always say it is so easy just to do what you want. Katie, he whispers, it is the hardest thing in the world.

She is cordial but chides him for talking in such a selfish way. People really should not take things so seriously, especially not love affairs. But, says Keating, what they were to each other—the moments he sat holding her, how she looked, how they sat on a bench in the snow—the things she never has regretted for a moment—those remain true forever, don't they? She says Keating was a nice boy. She must run, get back to Washington. She has no real self left. Keating has a remnant of honesty and selfhood—for now.

Roark joins Wynand on a months-long winter cruise on his yacht. Wynand had not expected Roark to agree, but he easily assents; construction for Cortlandt has started; other projects are several months away.

One evening, Wynand says he has embodied the selflessness Toohey preaches; yes, his motives have been money and other things, but he has lived to give voice to the opinions, desires, and tastes of the masses.. Roark says he did not think Wynand would ever admit that to himself. Why not, he rationalizes, he sold his life to the public and got a good price. Now, he thinks, he can use that power in any way he wants, for Roark and Dominique.

Roark says he now sees the principle behind the dean. He has come to understand the genuine selflessness of people who live entirely within others. The resulting emptiness was what Roark could not understand about people. Like Peter Keating, who is wondering what destroyed him and thinks he has been too selfish. In fact, he has betrayed himself in every way. All his achievements, fame, happiness have been in the eyes of others. He is what Roark now calls a "second-hander."

Second-handers accept anything but an independent man. Now, Roark understands and realizes how he chose his friends: a self-sufficient ego. When Wynand asks what led Roark to choose Wynand as his friend, Roark realizes he has said more than he intended. He answers: "That you weren't born to be a second-hander."

What Roark declines to mention is that the worst of all second-handers is the man who goes after power.

Back in New York, Roark sees a newspaper story

on Cortlandt Homes. Peter Keating is chief architect and Gordon L. Prescott and Gus Webb are associate architects. That evening, he goes to the Cortlandt site. The first building is up. It retains the economies and skeleton of Roark's design, but otherwise completely desecrates the building's integrity with arbitrary additions to the structure and façade.

No one really can say how it happened. Toohey had insisted on adding Prescott and Webb as associate designers to boost their reputations by association. Keating screamed that no changes are needed. Webb insisted on letting the associate architects assert their individuality.

Keating visits Roark to apologize. Roark believes Keating has done all he can. He does not want Keating to confess everything in public. He must leave things to Roark. However guilty Keating may be, Roark says, the real guilt is his. He has destroyed Keating by helping him, loading him with more success and fame than he could carry. This will be hard on you, Roark admits, but much harder on himself.

Roark asks Dominique's help. He lays out a scheme for her to draw the Cortlandt night watchman away. She will run out of gas and send him to the station a mile away. She must have an unchallengeable reason to be passing the site at that time. Then, when the watchman goes to the gas station, Dominique must run to a ditch and lie face down. She will know when to get up and run back to the car.

Dominique agrees, questioning nothing. When he leaves, Dominique realizes this was a test—and she has passed it. The fear of the world hurting Roark—even putting him in prison—is gone. She is free, at last. She can face anything, any outcome, and know the important thing is that they exist.

Dominique arranges the perfect alibi at a party in Long Island. She carries out the scheme at Cortlandt, lying face down when the explosion showers her with debris. She looks up to see the Cortlandt explosion filling the sky with girders and glass, and the flash reflected in windows across the East River.

She runs to her ruined car, slips in the front seat, grabs shards of glass to scratch her wrists, her arms, her face, her neck. Unwittingly, she slashes an artery. When the police arrive, she has only minutes to live.

Dominique wakes up in the hospital with Wynand there. The doctors had told him she would not survive. Wynand has Roark released on bail.

Wynand knows Roark blew up Cortlandt Homes—and is glad that Dominique became involved. She says to him: You wanted a chance now, after all these years? Yes, he does. Dominique says she loves him. If he sticks with the battle for Roark... Wynand says not to bribe him. This is not between Dominique and him. Not between Roark and him. For himself.

Roark tells Dominique he may spend years in prison. Yes, Dominique knows. He involved her in the plot to trap her. Otherwise, she would have come to Roark's apartment immediately and publicly revealed their relationship to share his fate. Now, she cannot; it would be declaring Roark guilty of the crime.

Roark says that now he knows she has lost her terrible fear of the world, what the world may do to Roark if he is convicted. If he must go to prison, he is counting on her to stay with Wynand, to save him. She promises she will.

And if Roark is acquitted? Yes, he says, she knows what that will mean. He has waited seven years for her to come to terms with the world. Dominique asks if Roark would sacrifice their relationship for Wynand. No, he says, his work, and Dominique, never can be sacrificed.

The public erupts in furious indignation at the crime. An egoistic architect blows up public housing for the poorest. His motive is not known. But it can be only selfish. A moral crime hideous without further inquiry. One man's ego against all that civilization has struggled to achieve. The whole roster of names made famous by Ellsworth Toohey weighs in to attack Roark.

The Wynand papers fight for Roark. Alvah Scarret is horrified. The *Banner* on the side of someone who destroyed a public housing project! Wynand himself writes editorial after editorial brilliantly defending Roark, the individual genius, arguing against the concept of self-sacrifice. Wynand tells himself he has lived and waited for this. What the *Banner* has done—and been—has been contemptible, but this will vindicate everything. The public will believe what Wynand tells them. By the time Roark comes to trial, no jury will dare convict him.

Wynand tells Toohey not to mention Roark or Cortlandt in his column. Toohey complies; he doesn't need to say anything. Articles and editorials by all his protégés skewer the *Banner* and Wynand for hypocrisy. The circulation of Wynand papers goes into free fall. It vanishes from newsstands.

Keating has refused to talk with the press. Toohey browbeats Keating into giving him the contract he signed with Roark. Toohey is delighted. He reads the agreement and confesses that it is sickening how Keating used Roark. "For one second," he feels like burning the paper. He won't burn it, he says, but for one moment he wanted to do so. He will send it to the district attorney.

What do you want to do to Roark? Keating asks. Toohey is disgusted with Keating; he has made clear for years what he wanted. He wants Roark in jail, confined, regimented, slapped, beaten.

Keating always knew that. Keating loved Roark, worshiped Roark, but always followed Toohey, whom he hated.

Keating is silent as Toohey berates him. Toohey was single-minded in his goal: to break individualism and independence in man's spirit so men could be ruled. He describes his many strategies, all disguised by the views he has promoted. Make men feel guilty for selfishness. Make them feel small. Make genius meaningless by elevating mediocrity, as he has done with his protégés.

Doesn't Keating see Toohey's philosophy all around him today? The final goal, the achievement of power, is collectivism—people without individual souls who serve. Doesn't Keating see that sweeping Europe in two different forms of totalitarianism? Why must Keating delude himself?

Toohey acknowledges that he has given Keating the speech that he never could give publicly. Toohey's role will be to rule. He will not be happy; that is not within his capacity. He will have such satisfaction as power gives.

Wynand returns from a business trip and fires Toohey and three editors for a column that attacked Roark. Toohey taunts him. The power Wynand sought through wealth was not real; Toohey's "impractical intellectuals," his power over opinion, the arts, ideas *are* real. He will be back and will run the *Banner*.

The editorial staff goes out on strike—all the "little people" hired on Toohey's recommendation. They demand the restoration of those fired and reversal of the *Banner*'s stand on Roark and the Cortlandt Homes bombing.

Wynand keeps publishing, working furiously, with Dominique's help. But the newspaper's quality plunges, circulation evaporates, advertisers flee. Public rage has shifted from Roark to Wynand. Wynand tells Roark he knows his efforts are hurting, not helping Roark. Roark agrees but urges Wynand to continue for his own sake.

Finally, the board of directors, including Mitch Layton, tell Wynand he must settle the strike and reverse his position. The choice is to settle or close the *Banner*. Wynand stands at his chair, listening, thinking of starting the *Banner*, building it, what it cost him, what it meant. He finally says all right. All he demands as a compromise is that Toohey not be reinstated.

He walks for hours through the night with the one thought that he did this to himself. He thought he was gaining power—running things around here. He thought the power he gained by pandering to the masses could be used to promote his ideals, but that was an illusion; he sees now that the masses are really his masters. His leash on them " is only a rope with a noose at both ends." He got the money and the yacht, but they got his soul; and he has sold them Howard Roark.

The next day's *Banner* reverses position: Roark is reprehensible, dangerous, unprincipled, and antisocial. Wynand says to himself: Howard, I wrote that editorial forty years ago. Anyone can be forgiven, he thinks, except the man who was not born to be a second-hander and became one.

That evening, Roark makes every effort to see Wynand, to say that what happened is not the final verdict on him. But Wynand rejects all contact.

Roark has rented a summer house in Monadnock Valley. He expects no one, but one evening Dominique arrives. The moment of their meeting leaves the seven years behind them. She tells him that now she fears nothing they can do to Roark or her. If he must go to prison, she will move there. She will visit him through a wire net. Dominique calls the police to come to investigate a theft that did not occur so that reporters will get the story that Mrs. Gail Wynand was with Mr. Roark, at his home, for breakfast.

The intimate, scandalous story hits the afternoon papers in New York.

Wynand reads the story. He tells Scarret to play it any way that he wishes. Scarret frantically urges Wynand to file for divorce immediately. Wynand tells him to go ahead and arrange it with his lawyer.

Wynand drives to the country house to see Dominique. He wants to know if this was her first time since their marriage. Yes, it was. But not the first time? No, Roark was Dominique's first lover; she tells Wynand the story of the quarry. Roark loved you? Yes. And yet he built this house for us? Yes. Wynand says he only wanted to know. Dominique cries that if he can take it like this, he had no right to become what he did.

Wynand forces himself to read every word of every newspaper with stories about the scandal Dominique has created. Scarret implores readers to forgive Wynand. The public responds with thousands of letters of sympathy and support for Wynand. Now, they will rebuild the old *Banner*. Yes, says Wynand, do it any way you wish.

In the courtroom for Roark's trial, Dominique sits with Roark's friends; Wynand enters alone at the last minute to sit in the last row. Roark has exercised many vetoes in jury selection; all the men on the jury are employed in industry or manual labor. From their hard faces, the prosecutor thinks Roark already has lost.

The prosecutor's opening statement focuses on the "monstrous" motive and ego of a man who would blow up public housing over a matter of his artistic tastes. He calls the night watchman, the police officer who discovered Roark at the site, and others to establish that Roark did dynamite Cortlandt. Then, in listless testimony, as if sleepwalking, Keating confirms that Roark designed the project on condition that it be built as he designed.

Roark rises for the defense. He stands before the court relaxed, a man without fear.

Roark speaks of man's first inventions and the innovators who created them, men of independent judgment and independent effort to create something new. For the creator, "His vision, his strength, his courage came from his own spirit. A man's spirit, however, is his self." But such men were condemned by the second-handers, who lived only through other men. Who thought as other men thought and sought their sanction for existing—in other men. Who embraced altruism, the ethic of selflessness, and denounced the men of independence in thought and action as "selfish."

The choice is independence or dependence. It is not, as altruism preaches, sacrifice to others or sacrifice others to self; both are forms of dependence. Rulers who seek power are just as dependent as those who sacrifice their interests.

Roark designed Cortlandt Homes when no other architect could do it. The impossibly low rents for the poor were made possible by his work. All he asked as payment was that the work be done his way, built exactly as he designed it. He was not paid. The owners of Cortlandt got what they bargained for; he did not. And that is why he dynamited Cortlandt.

If he must spend years in prison, now, he will consecrate those years to the America that was the triumph of individualism. He will give these years in memory of the greatest country on earth, the country of the individual, the innovator—and all that that came to mean to mankind.

The judge, a man with a face like a military officer, directs the jury. The prosecutor agrees that Roark has changed his plea: He committed the act but does not accept that it is a crime. The jury leaves to reach a verdict. Wynand and Dominique do not move. The rest of the audience slowly rises to await the decision, when there is a sharp rap, and they realize the jury is signaling to return. The judge asks Roark, the accused, to rise. At the same time, Wynand rises. What is the jury's verdict?

Not guilty. Roark's eyes first go not to Dominique but to Wynand. But Wynand has risen and is the first man to leave the courtroom. He knows it was a verdict on him as well as Roark.

Toohey wins his suit to be reinstated at the *Banner*. Wynand orders him to report for work before 9:00 p.m. Toohey sits at his desk, with Wynand watching. At the stroke of 9:00, the presses stop; the *Banner* is closed. Wynand felt it only fitting that he and Toohey be together at the end of the *Banner*.

Months later, Wynand asks Roark to his office. Roark hopes the pain of their estrangement is over. But when he steps into Wynand's office, he sees not the face of a stranger, but a face closed forever, never to be opened. There is no cure and no hope.

Wynand asks Roark to sign a contract for the Wynand building in Hell's Kitchen. It will be the tallest skyscraper in New York City and the last, given the direction of the world. The building will be occupied by the Wynand enterprises; Roark should consider the budget unlimited for anything he wants to build.

Wynand says the building had been intended to celebrate his life. But now, there is nothing to celebrate in his life, only in Roark's. Anything the building represents will come from Roark's spirit, not Wynand's. Roark immediately signs. Roark is not to communicate with Wynand about the building or anything else. Wynand's agent will handle all financial and other matters. It should not be necessary for Roark ever to see Wynand again. No, the world will not perish, says Roark, while it is capable of such things as this building.

Roark walks to the door, turns, and nods, holding it a moment too long, a farewell to Wynand. Wynand says: Build it to the spirit that is yours—and could have been mine. Some eighteen months later, on a spring day, Dominique walks into Hell's Kitchen. On the fence enclosing the construction site, there is a sign, "Howard Roark, Architect." It is the answer to the unfailing spirit and hope of Henry Cameron, who said that, in the end, Roark would make the answer for them all.

The new Wynand Building has risen into the sky as a skeleton of steel girders. The walls of glass are following the skeleton. Roark is at the top of the building. The supervisor knows how Dominique visits Roark, as she so often does. She steps onto an outdoor elevator of planks on the outside of the building and goes rising.

She rises over the common level of the city. She rises along the faces of the other skyscrapers. She rises above the roofs and the radio antennas. Now, she sees the rivers embracing Manhattan. She sees the ocean. She is rising above it all as it falls below her feet.

She looks up, then, and Roark has seen her. He waves.

And then she is above all of it. She looks up and sees nothing but the sea, the sky, and the figure of Howard Roark.

CAST OF CHARACTERS

Briefly described here are more than 50 characters in *The Fountainhead* that Ayn Rand named and one, called just the "dean," who remains in Roark's mind throughout the novel. Some characters appear only once, in one chapter, but if they are named they are here.

Ainsworth, Mr. and Mrs. Dale. Francon & Heyer have designed a palatial home for the couple. At a reception to celebrate its completion, Peter Keating, who designed it, and Guy Francon are in attendance. So is Dominique Francon, who has a *Banner* column on home decorating, and publishes a biting criticism of the house's architecture to make it a laughingstock. Guy is furious, unable to decide why his daughter does these things. She laughs.

Cameron, Henry. An innovator in modern architecture who led the profession at the turn of the 20th century, but by the time of the novel has been crushed by the national revival of neo-Classicism. He has almost no work, drinks constantly, and despairs of architecture's future. He is Roark's idol and model. When Roark leaves school, he goes to Cameron for work.

Bennett. He is a draftsman at Francon's firm who remains for many decades even as Keating rises through the firm and advances past him. When Keating heads the firm, Bennett is a principal colleague.

Bradley, Caleb. He gives Roark the commission to build a summer resort, Monadnock, in Pennsylvania. Only when the project is completed does it come to light that a dishonest clique of investors who wanted the project to fail hired Roark as the worst architect they could find. Monadnock becomes hugely popular and their scheme is revealed.

Brent, Sally. She is a popular gossip columnist at the *Banner* who gets fired when she defies Wynand's prohibition on publishing any stories or photographs relating to his wife, Dominique.

Carson, Dwight. An idealistic young writer, he is the first one Wynand breaks as part of his obsession to demonstrate that no idealism is real and degradation is inevitable in human life.

Clokey, Lancelot. A foreign correspondent for the *Banner*, he writes squalid books about what he was doing personally, often in bed, during great foreign events. Toohey makes his books bestsellers.

Cook, Lois. She is a writer of "poetic novels" made famous by the efforts of Ellsworth Toohey as a strategy for identifying literary genius with the common, the undistinguished. She is the author of a bestseller, "The Gallant Gallstone," which satirizes all individualism.

Cord, Anthony. With the example of Enright House attracting attention to Roark, Cord commissions Roark to build a fifty-five-story skyscraper. Designing skyscrapers is one of Roark's highest aspirations.

Davis, Tim. As a leading draftsman in Francon's firm, Davis becomes the target of Keating's first efforts at advancing by making friends. He manipulates Davis into arrangements that get him fired so Keating can take his place.

Dean. The dean at Stanton Institute expels Roark at the insistence of Prof. Peterkin, the teacher of design, and against the wishes of Roark's professors of structural engineering and mathematics. When he calls Roark to his office to offer him "another chance," they argue about "modern architecture." Roark does not return to the school.

Dunlop, Mrs. The wife of a wealthy couple planning a new home. Keating talks her into hiring Stengel, not Francon & Heyer, so Stengel will leave the firm, opening the way for Keating's next promotion.

Enright, Roger. A self-made millionaire, scornful of all public opinion and public pressure, he

commissions Roark to design the housing project
Enright House, one of Roark's pivotal early
projects. Enright becomes a friend and supporter
of Roark.

Fargo, John. A man of independent thinking who
gives Roark his first commission to design an
office building.

Francon, Guy. A partner in Francon & Heyer, the
leading New York architectural firm, building
his reputation on reverence for every and any
historical style and usually a mixture of them. He
hires Peter Keating right out of school.

Francon, Dominique. A woman of astonishing beauty,
she is Guy Francon's daughter. She falls in
love with Howard Roark, but she has grown up
with a horror of how true greatness, beauty, and
heroism are treated in the world. She can't stand
watching it happen to Roark. She would rather
destroy him, or herself, before it happens. She
first sets out to defeat Roark by winning clients
for Peter Keating, whom she despises but marries
to destroy her spirit. She later does that one better
by marrying Gail Wynand. When Wynand finally
discovers that his power-seeking has destroyed
him, and Roark always will be Roark, Dominique
loses her fears. She returns to Roark for whatever
happens.

Fougler, Jules. Toohey gets him hired as drama critic
at the *Banner* to promote plays of a quality that

destroys the concept of "brilliant" and genius.

Gowan, Jimmy. A self-made man in Connecticut sees the Heller house that Roark has designed and commissions Roark to build him a new gas station. It is a small commission, but only Roark's second.

Halsey, Catherine. The niece of Ellsworth Toohey, she is quietly in love with Peter Keating and the only thing in life that Keating wants for his own sake and happiness. Again and again, they decide to marry but concerns of power and prestige always overcome Keating.

Harding. He is managing editor of the *Banner*, but, when Toohey goes head-to-head with Wynand, publishing his column "One Small Voice" with an attack on Howard Roark—and publication is not blocked by Harding, Allen, and Falk of the top editorial staff while Wynand is traveling— the three editors along with Toohey are fired. This precipitates a devastating strike against the *Banner* that ends with its closing.

Heller, Austen. Columnist for the conservative *Chronicle*, a rival of the mighty "*Banner*," he is a defender of liberty who hates *Banner* publisher Gail Wynand. He discovers Roark as the only architect to build the house he always wanted and becomes a lifelong friend and ardent supporter of Roark.

Heyer, Lucius. The partner of Guy Francon, Heyer
is useful only for his old family connections by
the time Keating arrives. When Keating becomes
desperate to become Francon's partner, he finds
information to terrorize Heyer with blackmail.
Already recovering from a stroke and feeble,
Heyer is driven by Keating's vicious threats and
intimidation to have another stroke and die.

Holcombe, Ralston. A famous architect, head of the
American Guild of Architects, he is devoted to
Renaissance style as the only valid one.

Holcombe, Kiki. She is Ralston's wife, a leading
socialite, and maintains a prestigious salon for
architects.

Janss, Nathaniel. He wants to build a new store and
wants Roark for the job. But the store must have
"dignity" and feel comfortable to the public by
giving people what they know. Roark tries every
argument, but in the end, Janss is unconvinced.

Keating, Peter. A classmate of Roark's at Stanton,
who boards at Keating's mother's house while at
architecture school. Keating graduates first in his
class, with all honors, while Roark is expelled.
Keating rises through the firm of Francon &
Heyer to become New York's leading architect.
At every major step of his career, Keating
secretly goes to Roark to help him succeed, as
he did at Stanton. But he adheres to Ellsworth

Toohey who caters to his need for affirmation but uses Keating for his own ends. He fails to do the one thing in his life he really wants: to marry Catherine Halsey.

Keating, Mrs. Louisa. The mother of Peter Keating who starts his career exactly at the same time as Roark. She runs the boarding house where Roark stays for three years while in architecture school. She has manipulated Keating in every choice of his life.

Lansing, Kent. He is one of a group of investors seeking to build the Aquitania Hotel on Central Park South. After many bitter battles, he gets Roark hired as an architect only to see the project run out of money. Lansing works for years to get his "partners and brothers" out of the deal and finally calls Roark in triumph to resume work on the project.

Layton, Eva. Wife of Mitchell Layton.

Layton, Mitchell. A young multi-millionaire with inherited wealth, he is persuaded by Ellsworth Toohey to buy a big stake in the *Banner* as part of Toohey's surreptitious efforts to get in a position to control it. Like other wealthy men Toohey manipulates, Layton craves Toohey's opinion that despite being rich he has a "fine" (collectivist) soul.

Mallory, Steven. A brilliant young sculptor discovered by Roark, Mallory has been almost broken by the way the world has treated his work. Like Roark's architecture, Mallory's art is beautiful, heroic, projecting the best in man. Roark selects him to create a nude statue for the Stoddard Temple. The model is Dominique. He becomes a friend and supporter of Roark.

Mundy, Robert L. He is sent to Roark by Austen Heller. He has made his fortune but never forgotten how, growing up in Georgia, he was treated like a mere errand boy with no social standing. Now, he wants his own home like the grand mansion of the "best" people when he was growing up. Roark argues that by doing that he is letting them control him, but he has wanted a plantation-style house all his life. Roark does not get the commission.

Orsini, Pasquale. A worker in the Connecticut granite quarry owned by Guy Francon. When Roark is locked in a romantic duel with Dominique Francon, and she arranges for him to come to her bedroom to reset a broken tile, he sends Orsini. This is the act that drives Dominique to ride up and lash Roark's face with her crop.

Peterkin. Professor of design at Stanton, he insists that Roark be expelled for refusing to do assignments on historical style and submitting only his own ideas.

Pratt, Jessica. Attendee at one of Toohey's meetings of his councils of professionals whose careers he is promoting.

Prescott, Gordon L. A leading architect, chairman of the Council of American Builders, who thrives on imitation, "prestige," impressing others with his personality, and intimidating talk about architecture, he is a protégé of Ellsworth Toohey.

Roark, Howard. The hero of the novel, an architect of genius and an unshakably independent mind. As an innovator in an era that worships all historic styles, he is committed to doing his own work in his own way without compromise. He fights a decades-long battle against pervasive conformity and hostility to genius and genuine individualism. His buildings rise organically out of their site, have façades that express the function of the structure and each part of the interior, are open to air and light, and are superlatively efficient and economical. He becomes Dominique Francon's lover but waits many years as she is driven by her fear of what the world does to the best, the ideal, to men like Roark and to his work.

Sanborn, Mr. and Mrs. Whitford. They commission Roark to design their country home despite a furious disagreement between Whitford, who wants Roark because he loves a building Henry Cameron designed for him, and his wife, who wants something trendy. When the house is completed after endless changes, Mrs. Whitford refuses to live in it. But their son, Richard, withdrawn and unmotivated since college, declares he loves the house and stays to live in it.

Sanborn, Richard. The son of the Sanborns loves the house Roark has designed and is the only one who chooses to live in it.

Scarret, Alvah. The editor-in-chief of the *Banner*, he is a long-time colleague of Gail Wynand. He has accepted and completely internalized the lowest-common-denominator, pandering style that characterizes everything the *Banner* does and has made it a vulgar success. He stands by Wynand till the very end.

Shlinker, Ted. He is chief rival of Keating for head of the graduating class at Stanton. He is the first of many competitors in life that Keating must beat to preserve his sense of superiority.

Slottern, Homer. A department store owner and advertising client of the *Banner*, he is controlled by Toohey and used by him to try to destroy the *Banner*.

Slottern, Renee. She is Homer's wife and attends the Toohey meeting that becomes a long discussion of why all freedom requires compulsion and the only complete freedom is complete compulsion.

Snyte, John Erik. He heads a firm with an eclectic

approach to architecture, with his draftsmen nicknamed for different historical periods. Urgently needing work, Roark accepts a job with him and is nicknamed "Modernism." When Austen Heller, the columnist and crusader for political liberty, asks the firm to design his home, Roark's is the core drawing that is combined with those of the other draftsmen into a mishmash. Heller sees enough of Roark in the drawing, so that he cries out in frustration that this is it but isn't it. Somehow, it just lacks integrity. Roark seizes a pencil and slashes through the beautiful watercolor to recreate what he designed. Snyte fires Roark but Heller hires him.

Stengel. He is Chief Designer in Francon's office because Francon no longer does any drawing.
  He blocks Keating's advancement in the office until Keating gets rid of him.

Stoddard, Hopton. A wealthy businessman under the influence of Ellsworth Toohey, he is worried about his worthiness for salvation. Toohey convinces him to build a temple to the human spirit. Toohey tells Stoddard to hire Roark as architect and coaches Stoddard to convince Roark although Roark is not religious. Stoddard takes a one-year pilgrimage to religious sites. When he returns, Toohey convinces him that the completed temple is a desecration. *The Banner* leads a public campaign to portray Roark as attacking religion. At a trial, Roark loses his case against Stoddard and his reputation is ruined by the scandal.

Sutton, Joel. When Dominique sets out to take potential commissions away from Roark, Sutton is the first client she convinces. He had been ready to sign the contract with Roark that afternoon, but now reneges.

Toohey, Ellsworth. The chief villain of the novel. He lives to destroy Howard Roark because independence and genius are inimical to the "common man," the "masses," "equality," "humility," and sacrifice at the very deepest level. His role as an expert in architecture, a columnist for the *Banner* newspaper, and influential creator of groups of followers enables him to dream of controlling the *Banner* and gaining unlimited power to become one of the rulers of a selfless, "equal" world of the common man. He has enormous influence over Keating.

Weidler. He fights a battle with his directors to hire Roark to do their bank building. He thinks he has won but is distressed when the directors ask Roark for "one small compromise" that changes the façade of the building Roark designed. Roark refuses the commission.

Wilmot, Mrs. Wayne. She is sent to Roark as a potential client but discovers he will not do the house in Tudor style.

Wynand, Gail. Raised amidst gangs and squalor in Hell's Kitchen, New York, Wynand has risen to the pinnacles of the newspaper world with the sole objective of gaining power over the public, to become the man who "runs things here," and amass great wealth and luxury. His chief creation is Wynand papers and their flagship, the New York City giant, the *Banner*. He believes he has achieved total power but has become so jaded and unmotivated that he considers killing himself. When Ellsworth Toohey manipulates him into meeting Dominique, he falls profoundly in love and knows happiness for the first time. When searching for an architect to design for her the perfect house, he finds Howard Roark. Roark becomes the single greatest encounter and most important person in his life.

Our Work

Publications: From graphic novels to textbooks to pocket guides, our books are available in multiple formats and languages.

Narrative Videos: From animation to comedic features, our productions include Draw My Life videos and graphic novel-style compilations.

Educational Resources: Online courses, podcasts, webinars, campus speaking tours, living-history presentations, and campus activism projects are among the wealth of ways we educate students of all ages about reason, achievement, individualism, and freedom.

Student Programs: Our Atlas Advocates are eager, curious, and thoughtful students who meet for monthly book club discussions, and Richard Salsman, Ph.D.'s Morals & Markets webinar course; Our Atlas Intellectuals are adults who meet monthly to bring Ayn Rand's philosophy to bear on current events and real-world topics, curated by Stephen Hicks, Ph.D.

Commentaries: In addition to educational resources, our website offers commentaries on a wide range of political, cultural, and personal topics and events.

The Atlas Society is a 501(c)(3) non-profit organization, supported exclusively by private donors.